The Evangelical Landscape

List of Contributors

Mark A. Noll, McManis Professor of Christian Thought at Wheaton College, has authored, edited, or co-edited a variety of books including *Religion and American Politics: From the Colonial Period to the 1980s* (Oxford, 1990), *A History of Christianity in the United States and Canada* (Eerdmans, 1992), and *The Scandal of the Evangelical Mind* (Eerdmans, 1994), some of the arguments of which are set out in his chapter.

Bruce Shelley, Senior Professor of Church History at Denver Seminary, has authored, edited, or co-edited a variety of books including *Evangelicalism in America* (Eerdmans, 1967), *Church History in Plain Language* (Word, 1982), and *The Consumer Church* (InterVarsity, 1992).

Timothy L. Smith, retired Professor of History and Director of the Program in American Religious History at the Johns Hopkins University, has authored, edited, or co-edited a variety of books including *Revivalism and Social Reform* (Abingdon, 1957), *Whitefield and Wesley on the New Birth* (Johns Hopkins, 1980), and *The Promise of the Spirit* (Bethany, 1980).

Garth M. Rosell, Professor of Church History at Gordon-Conwell Theological Seminary, has authored, edited, or co-edited a variety of books including *American Christianity* (Eerdmans, 1986), *The Memoirs of Charles G. Finney* (Zondervan, 1989), and *The Millionaire and the Scrublady* (Zondervan, 1990).

The Evangelical Landscape

Essays on the American Evangelical Tradition

Edited by Garth M. Rosell

A Division of Baker Book House Co
Grand Rapids, Michigan 49516

©1996 by Garth M. Rosell

Published by Baker Books
a division of Baker Book House Company
P.O. Box 6287, Grand Rapids, MI 49516-6287

Printed in the United States of America

Library of Congress Cataloging-in-Publication Data

The evangelical landscape : essays on the American evangelical
    tradition / edited by Garth M. Rosell.
        p.   cm.
    Includes bibliographical references and index.
    ISBN 0-8010-2084-0 (pbk.)
    1. Evangelicalism—United States. I. Rosell, Garth.
BR1642.U5E87   1996
277.3′082—dc20   96-21170

For information about academic books, resources for Christian leaders, and all new releases available from Baker Book House, visit our web site:

http://www.bakerbooks.com/

Contents

Introduction:
The Evangelical Vision

On the morning of May 4, 1943, as the delegates to the Constitutional Convention gathered at the La Salle Hotel in Chicago to organize the new National Association of Evangelicals (NAE), Harold John Ockenga approached the podium to deliver the presidential address.[1] "I believe that the United States of America has been assigned a destiny comparable to that of ancient Israel," the young pastor of Boston's Park Street Church declared to the 148 leaders who had assembled from across the country. "God has prepared this nation with a vast and united country, with a population drawn from innumerable blood streams, with a wealth which is unequaled, with an ideological strength drawn from the traditions of classical and radical philosophy, with a government held accountable to law as no other government except Israel has ever been, and with an enlightenment in the minds of the average citizen which is the climax of social development." He has

---

1. For the early development of the National Association of Evangelicals see Arthur H. Matthews, *Standing Up, Standing Together: The Emergence of the National Association of Evangelicals* (Carol Stream, Ill.: National Association of Evangelicals, 1992); Joel A. Carpenter, ed., *A New Evangelical Coalition: Early Documents of the National Association of Evangelicals* (New York and London: Garland, 1988); and Elizabeth Evans, *The Wright Vision: The Story of the New England Fellowship* (Lanham, Md.: University Press of America, 1991).

done so for the unquestionable purpose of spreading "the knowledge of God" and the "truth [of] the Gospel" throughout the world.[2]

Yet, Ockenga continued, America "is passing through a crisis which is enmeshing western civilization. Confusion exists on every hand. We are living in a very difficult and bewildering time." The "kingdom of hell," with its "indifference to God," its rampant "secularism," and its preoccupation with fleshly interests, is "at hand." "The hour has arrived when the people of this nation must 'think deeply or be damned.' We must examine our direction, our condition and our destiny. We must recognize that we are standing at the crossroads and that there are only two ways that lie open before us. One is the road of the rescue of western civilization by a re-emphasis on and revival of evangelical Christianity. The other is a return to the Dark Ages of heathendom which powerful force is emerging in every phase of world life today." There is "a 'now or never' urgency in this matter. The time to strike is here. The iron is hot. The door is open. The need is great." Indeed, the world is waiting "for the clear cut, definite, sane and progressive leadership which can inaugurate a new era for Christian influence and effectiveness."

To many of the weary warriors of the bitter Fundamentalist-Modernist battles, which had been fought so valiantly throughout the previous decades, Ockenga's challenge must have come as a breath of fresh air.[3] Rather than a continuation of the strategy of withdrawal, here was a challenge to re-engage the culture and its institu-

2. Harold John Ockenga, "Christ for America," in *United Evangelical Action*, vol. 2, no. 1 (May 4, 1943), 3–4, 6. Subsequent quotations from this address are taken from this source.

3. On the Fundamentalist-Modernist controversy see George M. Marsden, *Fundamentalism and American Culture: The Shaping of Twentieth-Century Evangelicalism, 1870–1925* (New York: Oxford University Press, 1980).

tions. Instead of retreat, here was a call to advance the gospel throughout the world. In place of discouragement and fear, here was new hope for spiritual power and refreshment. Rather than endless argumentation, division, and fragmentation, here at last was the possibility of united evangelical action.[4]

There is a sense in which Harold John Ockenga's stirring address, so enthusiastically received by most of the delegates, became a kind of manifesto for the resurgent evangelicalism that came to dominate mid-twentieth-century America. Rooted in the rich soil of American Puritanism, this "New Evangelicalism," as Ockenga would later call it, sought—as had its eighteenth- and nineteenth-century predecessors—to join together Christians of many denominations in the spread of biblical Christianity throughout the world. United by a common authority (the Bible), a common experience (conversion), a common conviction (that salvation is to be found only in the atoning work of Christ) and a common mission (worldwide evangelization), these New Evangelicals set out to recapture the culture for Christ.

Centers of learning, such as those universities that had been largely abandoned by a generation of evangelical students in favor of Christian colleges and Bible schools, must be re-engaged. "We have a need of new life from Christ in our nation," Ockenga was convinced, and "that need first of all is intellectual." Unless "the Church can produce some

4. For a listing of the broad range of published studies on evangelicalism three bibliographies are especially helpful: Norris A. Magnuson and William G. Travis, *American Evangelicalism: An Annotated Bibliography* (West Cornwall, Conn.: Locust Hill Press, 1990); Edith L. Blumhofer and Joel A. Carpenter, *Twentieth-Century Evangelicalism: A Guide to the Sources* (New York: Garland, 1990); and Robert D. Shuster, James Stambaugh, and Ferne Weimer, *Researching Modern Evangelicalism* (New York: Greenwood, 1990). See also the excellent bibliographical essay by Leonard I. Sweet, ed., *The Evangelical Tradition in America* (Macon, Ga.: Mercer University Press, 1984), 1–86.

thinkers who will lead us in positive channels our spiral of degradation will continue downward." Furthermore, he continued, "there is great need in the field of statesmanship." Where are the political leaders "in high places of our nation," he asked, with "a knowledge of and regard for the principles of the Word of God?" The need is "even more evident in the business world," he continued, where models of Christian integrity have become such a rarity.

Most of all, he concluded, "there must be a new power in personal life. Unless this message of salvation which we hold to be the cardinal center of our Christian faith really does save individuals from sin, from sinful habits, from dishonesty, impurity and avarice, unless it keeps them in the midst of temptation, what good is it? Christians today are altogether too much like the pagan and heathen world both in actions and in life." What the church needs most at the present time and in the future "is *saints,* great Christians—Christ loving men and women." Only out of such a company "can a new vision grow for the future of America." Our salvation is to be found in neither "a new economic-social order nor a political new deal" but rather in "Bible Christianity, with Christ the leader and eternity in view."

After years of discouragement, many believers seemed ready and eager to march under the new evangelical banner. For nearly two decades, during the 1940s and 1950s, leaders of the burgeoning New Evangelical movement continued to challenge their followers to spread the influence of biblical Christianity to every corner of the society. As the movement grew, spurred in large measure by the powerful ministry of Youth for Christ and through the remarkable revivals that marked the early 1950s, some observers such as the editor of the NAE's journal *United Evangelical Action,* were ready to proclaim "the defeat of Liberalism" in 1950 and the arrival of "the Evangelical Year" in 1951. The "revival of religion that is underway in

America" has broken all of "Billy Sunday's mighty records of attendance." Billy Graham "headed the most spectacular demonstration of revival power." Add to this "the multitude of God-blessed ambassadors of the cross, such as Merv Rosell, Jack Shuler, John R. Rice, Bob Jones, Hyman Appelman, and the growing power of Christ for America under the leadership of Horace Dean and it becomes evident that we are witnessing one of the greatest outpourings of the Spirit in the nation's history."[5]

More than fifty million Americans, by some estimates, were eventually drawn into the evangelical ranks as a result of these and subsequent efforts. For nearly two decades, the vision that Ockenga had so clearly proclaimed to the delegates at the Constitutional Convention provided shape and direction for a remarkably cohesive movement. By the 1960s, however, it seemed apparent that the familiar evangelical landscape was beginning to change. While encouraging evidence of God's renewing work continued to abound—from the worldwide ministry of Billy Graham to charismatic renewal within many churches—the disquieting challenges of radical theology, declining membership in America's mainline churches, the pervasive relativism of a postmodern world and a growing preoccupation with the "self," to name but a few, seemed at least in some quarters to have dimmed the evangelical vision, fostered institutional fragmentation, and encouraged new strategies of withdrawal from the culture and its institutions.

Whether or not such an analysis is accurate, there can be little question that evangelicalism in the last half of this century has become increasingly difficult to understand and describe. Indeed, there seems to be a continuing need to examine the nature and the direction of the movement

5. *United Evangelical Action*, July 15, 1950, and January 1, 1952.

if we hope to learn from its failures and recover its strengths. It is for this reason that the Ockenga Institute of Gordon-Conwell Theological Seminary organized a conference in 1990 to examine some of these themes. Three distinguished historians of American evangelicalism—Mark Noll, Bruce Shelley, and Timothy Smith—were invited to explore with the seminary community various aspects of what was called the evangelical landscape. Not only were their lectures well received by faculty and students alike, but also they have continued to foster discussion on our campus regarding the shape and direction of contemporary evangelicalism. By making these lectures available to a broader audience, it is our hope that those conversations can be extended beyond our campus as well.

Since the chapters were originally delivered as lectures, the reader will quickly recognize their oral rather than written characteristics. This means, of course, that there are no footnotes. However, at the end of each chapter, those who are interested will find a list of suggested readings for further study and reflection. Special thanks are due to Kurt Peterson for preparing them.

I am pleased that Baker Book House has agreed to make these lectures available to a wider audience. Allan Fisher, Jim Weaver, and the rest of the Baker staff have been of enormous help and encouragement in bringing the publication to completion. A special word of appreciation should also be given to President Robert E. Cooley, Dean Kenneth L. Swetland, and the rest of my colleagues at Gordon-Conwell Theological Seminary for their continued support of the project. It is our hope that the publication of this little volume will stimulate further discussion of a movement with which many of us identify but too few of us understand.

Garth M. Rosell
South Hamilton, Massachusetts

1

The Evangelical Mind

Mark A. Noll

As modern evangelicals, we are spiritual descendants of the Puritans. Yet the Puritan kind of comprehensive thinking under God, the sort of mind shaped to its furthest reaches by Christian influences, we modern evangelicals do not enjoy. At least we do not enjoy it very much, and we do not enjoy very much of it. Moreover, as evangelicals in the United States we have not had this kind of Christian mind, this breadth of Christian thinking, for most of our national history. We are, and for several generations have been, in the position once described by Harry Blamires: "In contradistinction to the secular mind, no vital Christian mind plays fruitfully, as a coherent and recognizable influence, upon our social, political, or cultural life. . . . Except over a very narrow field of thinking, chiefly touching questions of strictly personal conduct, we Christians in the modern world accept, for the purpose of mental activity, a frame of reference constructed by the secular mind and a set of criteria reflecting secular evaluations. There is no Christian mind; there is no shared field of discourse in which we can move at ease

13

as thinking Christians by trodden ways and past established landmarks. . . . Without denying the impact of important isolated utterances, one must admit that there is
no packed contemporary field of discourse in which writ-
ers are reflecting Christianly on the modern world and
modern man." Blamires may overstate the case slightly,
but his major point—that British and American Christians by and large have lacked a flourishing intellectual
culture—is painfully accurate.

I would like to explore with you some aspects of the
evangelical mind in the twentieth century. To do so it will
be necessary to take our bearings briefly from the broader
history of the church, but most of our attention will be focused on developments of the last two generations or so
in which evangelical thinking has made a remarkable yet
still incomplete comeback. For the task of gaining a perspective on the recent past, however, what could be better
in a New England setting than casting our minds back to
the original European settlers of this region?

Taking Our Bearings from Church History

New England Puritanism and its British counterpart had
one distinguishing characteristic: its effort to unite the
theology of the Reformation with a comprehensive view
of the world. From the testimony of the continental Reformers and their own study of Scripture, the Puritans
were convinced that a vital personal religion is the well-
spring of all earthly good. They were equally convinced
that all aspects of life, whether political, social, cultural,
economic, or ecclesiastical, need to be brought into sub-
jection to God. This Puritan synthesis of heart religion
and comprehensive concern for all areas of life drew upon
the continental heritage of Protestantism; but it was, in its
fullest expression, the unique contribution of the English-

speaking Reformation to the development of American civilization.

The key thing for us is to see how much Puritanism constituted a mind, as well as a theological position, a stance toward the church, and a style of spirituality. The Puritans were perhaps wrong on particular issues. In my opinion, for example, Puritans were altogether too confident that their specific interpretations of the Bible could be equated with the message of Scripture itself. They were just as blameworthy when they resorted to coercion to force those particular interpretations upon Quakers, Roman Catholics, Baptists, and others who questioned their wisdom. Without making light of such failures, it is still possible to say that the glory of the Puritans was to believe what they believed and do what they did as parts of a self-consciously comprehensive intellectual effort. As a result, with Puritans like John Milton and John Bunyan we can observe an identifiably Puritan aesthetic; with rulers like John Winthrop, William Bradford, and Oliver Cromwell we find the rudiments of an identifiable Puritan politics; from many ministers and magistrates we discover a well-articulated Puritan social theory; in addition, the Puritans worked out particular views on work, business ethics, recreation, sexual love, and many other spheres of what we now often call secular life. These manifestations of Christian thinking were rooted in the Puritans' theology, ecclesiology, and piety; but they went well beyond these more explicitly religious concerns. What we see among Puritans, in other words, are the fruits of a Christian mind.

Since the time of the Puritans, however, evangelical efforts to think comprehensively, under God, about the world have been far more sporadic. Given the entire history of Christianity in America, it might be a temptation to suggest that neglecting the life of the mind has been a valuable thing for believers. Comprehensive and coherent Christian thinking has rarely played a major part in the evangelical life of America. Our emphasis has been much more on activity, energetic attention to problem solving, and a preference for the accomplishments of know-how. But, some might ask, has not this situation been for the good? For example, while European churches over the last centuries have descended into learned and lifeless liberalism, and while America's mainline churches—with their aspirations to learned culture—have experienced increasing difficulties over the last decades, America's self-confessed evangelicals have become numerous, vocal, visible, and influential. While others were taking care of the thinking, we evangelicals became activists in missions and reform. Would not the state of the church around the world today suggest that we have chosen the better way?

There is a kernel of truth to such a conclusion. Hard intellectual labor has not always led to a healthy church. Sometimes, in fact, the pursuit of learning has been a means to escape the claims of the gospel or the requirements of God's law. It is also true that vital Christianity has existed, at least for brief periods, without a noticeable increase in seriousness about the intellect. Yet, the picture over the long term is different. Where Christian faith is securely rooted, where it penetrates deeply into a culture to change individual lives and redirect institutions, where it continues for more than a generation as a living testimony to the grace of God—in these situations, we almost invariably find Christians ardently cultivating the intellect for the glory of God.

Two generalizations concerning Christian thinking are amply illustrated in the lengthy annals of Christian history, including the history of Christianity in America: first, dynamic Christian movements that have exerted a long-lasting influence have always involved the evangelization of the mind; and second, failure to take the mind captive for Christ invariably leads to the weakening or the collapse of Christian vitality. These generalizations prove as true for the early church as for the history of monasticism in the Middle Ages, for the Pietist quickenings of the eighteenth century as for the confessional traditions arising out of the Reformation. The benefits to be gained from the evangelization of the mind are illustrated nowhere better than once again in this very region—in particular with the record of Jonathan Edwards, New England's greatest gift to the world of Christian thought.

If we had time to rehearse the career of Jonathan Edwards, it would show how fruitful it can be to love the Lord with the whole mind. His works on revival helped the church pick its way through complicated questions about the place of emotion in religious life. His theological books have helped many to work through questions about the nature of original sin and of the human will. In more recent years his philosophical writings have stimulated much serious reflection. Yet Edwards's career shows us something more: it is not simply advantageous to love the Lord with the mind; it is also good, it is sweet, it is holy, it is beautiful, it is honoring to God. In a word, the last reward to be had from the exercise of a Christian mind is to know God better, and that reward requires no other justification.

What Edwards shows us is why our minds are important, why our attitude toward knowledge is of central Christian significance. Who, after all, made the world of nature, and then made possible the development of sciences through which we find out more about nature? Who formed the universe of human interactions, and so provided the raw material of politics, economics, sociology, and history? Who is the source of harmony, form, and narrative patterns, and so lies behind all artistic and literary possibilities? Who created the human mind in such a way that it could grasp the realities of nature, of human interactions, of beauty, and so made possible the theories on such matters by philosophers and psychologists? Who, moment by moment, sustains the natural world, the world of human interactions, and the harmonies of existence? Who maintains the connections between what is in our minds and what is in the world beyond our minds? The answer in every case is the same: God did it, and God does it.

When we give our minds to the task of learning about any aspect of the world, the result will also have immense practical benefits for the church, making it better, wiser, and more efficient. But these benefits are all secondary. What matters most in coming to know the world better is that in so doing we come to know God better. That truth is what drove Edwards to develop a Christian mind, even as it had driven the Reformers and many other Christians throughout history in their study of the world. That truth is the final justification for developing a Christian mind.

With that brief historical background, we may now turn to the recent history of the evangelical movement. Over the last half-century and more, a significant number of American evangelicals have once again begun seriously to pursue the life of the mind as a Christian task. Breakthroughs in this effort have been few and triumphs modest, but the effort has gone on long enough to offer some genuine reasons for encouragement, as well as some sobering realities about the task that is still set before us.

Transforming Forces in Education and Values

From a historian's point of view, the most remarkable thing about these recent ventures in evangelical thought is that they exist at all. Two of the most salient episodes in evangelical history from the turn of the century both might have suggested that the pursuit of Christian thinking by evangelicals had become a hopeless task. The first of these was the transformation of the American university at the end of the nineteenth century, which saw the evangelicals who had dominated college life to that time utterly vanquished. The second was the Fundamentalist-Modernist controversy that saw a wholesale adoption of anti-intellectual convictions by the heirs of the evangelicals. Since each of these earlier episodes continues to affect evangelical intellectual efforts, they are both worth brief attention before we look at the somewhat more hopeful developments of the last half-century.

Few historical events have been more important for the evangelical mind than the reorganization of American colleges at the end of the nineteenth century. The years from 1865 to 1900 constituted a distinct era of transition for American higher education. When Charles Eliot became president of Harvard in 1869, he set that influential institution on a course of innovation and expansion. The Johns Hopkins University, founded in 1876, exercised leadership in the establishment of graduate education. Other major changes were also under way: new universities like Cornell, Chicago, and Stanford were founded; older private colleges like Yale, Princeton, and Columbia were transformed into universities with the addition of graduate and professional schools; major state universities like Michigan and Wisconsin grew up almost overnight in the Midwest.

In almost every way imaginable, the new university undercut the traditional values of Christian higher education in America. That education, though deeply flawed, did attempt a reconciliation between Christian faith and the world of learning. Between the Civil War and World War I, that reconciliation became a thing of the past. Excess capital generated by the industrialists after the Civil War arose from a widespread exploitation of new scientific technology. This excess wealth was generated, furthermore, by individuals who had largely laid aside the constraints of Christian altruism that America's old Christian-cultural synthesis had tried to inculcate. American industrialists, to one degree or another, seemed to have favored the kind of social Darwinism popularized by Herbert Spencer.

One of the reasons this new class of wealthy Americans funded education was to encourage more of the practical science and managerial theory coming from the new universities and less of the moralism coming from the old colleges with solid Christian rootings. Whether through the direct influence of the industrialists or not, clergymen were replaced by businessmen on college boards of trustees, and ministers were replaced as college presidents by educators alert to management ideas and the demands of the new science. These new presidents, in turn, focused much more attention on scholarship than on orthodoxy. Furthermore, the new scholarship that these presidents encouraged had been "liberated" from the old orthodoxies that once dominated American colleges. The new work was naturalistic in science and pragmatic in philosophy; in turn—and this brings the circle full—the new naturalistic science and the new pragmatic philosophy encouraged industrial giantism by providing training and technique to the capitalists while at the same time offering few criticisms of the new industrial wealth.

Against this combination of new money, social Darwinism, and naturalistic science, the old synthesis of evangelical convictions and American ideals stood almost no chance. The collapse of that synthesis signaled the collapse of the effort to construct an evangelical mind in America. From the point of view of the new university, the effort to view knowledge whole was abandoned under the assumption that discrete parts of truth, discovered through empirical science, could stand on their own. The effort to integrate religious faith with learning was abandoned under the assumption that the pursuit of science carried with it no antecedent commitments to any worldview. The quality of Christian thinking may not have been high in antebellum America, but at least it was there. With the rise of the new university, there was an almost complete abandonment of even the effort to develop a distinctly Christian mind.

The general sense of intellectual weakness that evangelicals displayed during the transformation of the American university was heightened by the events of the Fundamentalist-Modernist period. Again in this episode we encounter an ambiguity, for there are also many good things that must be said about the Fundamentalists of the early twentieth century. At a time when naturalism threatened religion, when relativism assaulted social morality, when intellectual fashions were turning the Bible into a book of merely antiquarian interest, Fundamentalists said exactly what needed to be said about the supernatural character of religion, the objectivity of Christian morality, and the timeless validity of Scripture. At the same time, however, Fundamentalism also acted to confirm evangelicals in certain features of nineteenth-century religious life that had anything but a favorable effect on the mind. Mention of these does not constitute a final evaluation of Fundamentalism as a whole, but serves only to show how the course Fundamentalism took made it more difficult for evangelicals to develop a Christian mind.

The most obvious Fundamentalist attack on the mind came in response to the drift of American academic life. With naturalistic or secular ideas now established as leading guides of the university, the Fundamentalist tendency was to attack learning in general as a preserve of evil. The Fundamentalist period witnessed a renewed suspicion of philosophical and theological speculation among evangelicals, an increased fear of European thought of whatever sort, and a reluctance to engage modern minds in dialogue. For their part, evangelicals advanced alternative forms of reasoning as well as alternative conclusions about the world. Thus, works like the Scofield Reference Bible and the twelve-booklet series of *The Fundamentals* marked a flowering of realistic, commonsensical, and democratic thinking. But this very flowering drove the wedge even deeper between the received habits of evangelical thought and the standards almost universally accepted in the changing academic world at large.

To illustrate that disengagement, it is helpful to look at the contrasting conceptions of science that divided Fundamentalists from the universities. Even as American Fundamentalists solidified their alliance with the common-sense science of the early nineteenth century, a newer form of scientific explanation had begun to excite the imagination of pioneering intellectuals. The scientific worldview of an earlier day—of Bacon, Newton, Locke, and the Scottish common-sense philosophers—was beginning to give way to forms of scientific explanation first associated with Charles Darwin, but soon the common possession of the academic community in general.

The explanations of the older science no longer sufficed for the scientists of the twentieth century, but Fundamentalists continued to insist upon their necessity for a proper understanding of God and the world. The older science was mechanistic, its model the carefully constructed watch; the newer science was organic, its model the growing plant. The older science was static and antithetical, scientific conclusions were fixed and could be stated dogmatically, once and for all; the newer science was developmental and synthetic, scientific conclusions were expected to change over time and often included considerable ambiguity. The older science was realistic, our minds took reality from the external world; the new science was often idealistic, our minds shaped perceptions of the world. The older science was commonsensical, it made much of appeals to the ordinary perceptions of ordinary people; the newer science was esoteric, it talked of straight lines curving deep in space, of matter changed into energy, and of particles with negative weight—all notions violating the common sense of ordinary people.

The great problem for American evangelicals in adjusting to newer scientific explanations was that they first came to American attention through the work of Charles Darwin. Darwinists seemed to have no interest in harmonizing the latest scientific discoveries with Christian truth. In fact, Darwinists were often even materialists, denying the Christian idea of the soul; they could be agnostic, questioning the knowability of God; they argued for randomness and chance in nature, and so denied God's design of the world.

In reaction to these anti-Christian tendencies, Fundamentalists rejected the work of Darwin and the Darwinists; but in so doing they also tended to reject the newer modes of scientific explanations with which Darwinism was associated. The earlier marriage between evangelical belief and the science of the early nineteenth century made that rejection easy. To the evangelical wedded to the old science, the newer science itself was condemned as speculative, metaphysical, and insecurely based on directly observable facts. To the Fundamentalist the newer science was linked too closely to the impieties of the Darwinists. The result of rejecting both the newer science and what were perceived as anti-Christian applications was a nearly total disengagement between Fundamentalists and the scientific intellectual culture of twentieth-century America.

The Fundamentalist movement also rekindled nationalistic fervor for America. Evangelicals had grown accustomed to thinking that revival and religiously-directed reform were the only ways to save the country. In the process, however, some evangelicals had lost the ability to discriminate between the good of the country and the good of the faith. As a result some evangelicals regarded the Fundamentalist-Modernist controversy as a last-ditch defense of not only the gospel, but America as well. To preserve one was to preserve the other. From Fundamentalism, modern evangelicals have learned that to defeat modernism and immorality was to save not only souls for the kingdom but also a future for the United States. For our purposes, the problem with this aspect of Fundamentalism is that it reinforced dubious nineteenth-century assumptions about the close bonds between Christian faith and American ideals. Wherever those assumptions were reinforced, reaction rather than thought was the inevitable result.

The Fundamentalist era also strengthened evangelical individualism. Theological conservatives who left the major denominations were thrown on their own resources for maintaining the beliefs, practices, and institutions to which they were committed. Theological conservatives who stayed in denominations were forced to develop strategies for survival that also emphasized resourcefulness and strength of individual effort. The result in both cases was to further underscore another dubious conviction of the nineteenth-century evangelical heritage: to advance the kingdom of God it was necessary to rely primarily upon the ingenuity and resourcefulness of individual action. The end result for intellectual life was to underscore the earlier suspicion of tradition, to restrict the possibility of learning from others, and so to hamper the life of the mind.

Whatever else we may say of it, the populist character of Fundamentalism had a negative effect on the life of the mind. In what had now become traditional American fashion, Fundamentalism encouraged the translation of intellectual issues into political struggles. It encouraged evangelical leaders to solve problems by enlisting larger and larger numbers of followers rather than by carefully analyzing Scripture or the world. The net result has been described by historian Nathan Hatch in these words: "Let me suggest somewhat whimsically that the heritage of fundamentalism was to Christian learning for Evangelicals like Chairman Mao's 'Cultural Revolution' [was] for the Chinese. Both divorced a generation from mainline academia, thus making reintegration [into the larger world of learning] a difficult, if not bewildering task."

From the perspective of 1930, the evangelical mind in America looked dead, dead, dead, as many articulate commentators, including H. Richard Niebuhr, thought it was. Not only were the nation's universities alien territory for evangelicals, but Fundamentalists, the most visible evangelicals, had made a virtue of their alienation from the world of learned culture. Appearances, however, as often before in the history of the church, proved deceptive. For at the apparent nadir of evangelical thought in America, new signs of life were stirring, all of which contributed to a more positive approach to Christian thinking and the development of an evangelical mind.

Stirrings of New Life

Four parallel developments in the 1930s and 1940s prepared the way for these improvements, each of which pushed toward greater balance between active piety and

NADIR ?

intellectual sophistication. The first and most dramatic story was the emergence within American Fundamentalism of younger leaders seeking an intellectually responsible expression of the Christian faith. Fundamentalist retrenchment and disengagement in the 1920s seemed to signal the end of intellectual vitality. Before too long, however, ambitious young Fundamentalists were finding sectarianism and separation an obstruction to Christian faith and practice. Harold John Ockenga (1905–1985), at various times the president of Fuller Seminary and Gordon-Conwell Theological Seminary, called for a "new Evangelicalism" that could value scholarship and take an active interest in society while maintaining traditional Protestant orthodoxy. E. J. Carnell (1919–1967) was only one of many who sought training at the nation's best graduate schools. After attending evangelical institutions (Wheaton College and Westminster Theological Seminary), he completed doctorates at both Harvard and Boston University before entering into a career of writing, teaching, and administration at the new Fuller Theological Seminary in California. Carl F. H. Henry (b. 1913), who expressed his concern for an intellectually responsible evangelicalism through teaching at Fuller and as the founding editor of *Christianity Today* (1956), called Fundamentalists to a new engagement with American society and a new concern for theological reflection. Together these and other like-minded leaders soon spoke for a significant number of theological conservatives who valued responsible education and an intellectually responsible expression of the faith.

The second element concerns theological conservatives who never became Fundamentalists. The major American denominations always contained individuals who valued the traditional confessions and who sought to exert a leavening restraint on the drift toward theological modernism that has characterized many groups in the twentieth century. For these individuals the significant development was finding "fundamentalists" who, like themselves, possessed confidence in a traditional understanding of Scripture, but who also valued well-considered theological argumentation. As tumult from the Fundamentalist-Modernist wars receded into the historical background, it became easier for these theological conservatives to reestablish lines of contact with evangelicals outside of their denominations.

The third development was one of assimilation. By the early twentieth century, European Protestants with strong attachment to confessions from the Reformation era had established significant communities in America. The largest of these were Lutheran. In spite of efforts by leaders like Carl Henry, however, connections between America's New Evangelicals and the Lutherans remained, and continue to be, somewhat tenuous. The situation was different with a smaller group of European confessionalists, the Dutch Reformed. During the 1930s and 1940s, members of the Christian Reformed Church, the denomination representing the most recent immigration from Holland, continued the process of Americanization that had started in earnest during World War I. Evangelicals offered these Dutch Reformed an important reference point as they moved closer to American ways. The Dutch, like the American evangelicals, confessed reliance upon the Scriptures and greatly valued practical spirituality. Although their standards of piety bore the impress of Europe (e.g., drinking and smoking were never automatically sinful as they were for many American evangelicals), they could appreciate the spirituality of American Pietists. As they grew closer to evangelical networks, the Dutch Reformed offered their American counterparts a heritage of serious academic work and experienced philosophical reasoning. In their native Holland, these Dutch Reformed had founded at the end of the nineteenth century a major center of higher education, the Free University of Amsterdam; they had made significant contributions to political theory and practice (their leader, Abraham Kuyper, was prime minister of the Netherlands from 1900 to 1905); and they enjoyed a full Christian participation in artistic and cultural life.

The most obvious link between these Dutch Reformed and American evangelicals came through their publishers. By the late 1940s, several firms in Grand Rapids, Michigan, a center of Dutch immigration, were publishing the books of Henry, Carnell, and other American evangelicals. Especially the William B. Eerdmans Company was aggressively seeking new authors and markets from the world of American evangelicals.

Eerdmans also played an important part in drawing a fourth strand of evangelical renewal into the American picture. Beginning in the 1930s, a number of British evangelicals—from the Church of England as well as from dissenting denominations—united in efforts to extend an evangelical influence in the universities. The cradle for this effort was the British InterVarsity Fellowship (IVF), the nursemaids of which were graduate students and young professors who were convinced of the intellectual integrity of evangelical faith. Led by preachers like Martin Lloyd-Jones, scholars like F. F. Bruce and David Wenham, and organizers like Douglas Johnson, these British evangelicals made significant progress in a relatively short period of time. Forceful yet dignified preaching missions to Oxford, Cambridge, and other universities established an evangelical presence and led to the conversion of undergraduates. By the end of the 1940s, the Theological Students Fellowship of IVF established Tyndale House in Cambridge to encourage evangelical study of the

Scriptures, and soon thereafter evangelicals began to gain research positions in major British universities. The British InterVarsity Press published many products of this renewed evangelicalism, often with Eerdmans as a co-sponsor or the American distributor. The printed word thus served as a medium linking British evangelicals to Americans of several varieties of postfundamentalists, mainline conservatives, and Americanizing confessionalists. In addition, by the 1950s, American evangelicals were regularly going across the Atlantic to pursue graduate work with scholars either holding a similar faith or open to its emphases at the British universities.

Parenthetically, it is important also to note the immense importance of another Briton for the life of the mind among twentieth-century American evangelicals. By a careful definition of the term, C. S. Lewis was not an evangelical; yet his work has constituted the most important body of intellectual stimulation for American evangelicals in our century. His defense of supernatural Christianity, his ability to exploit learned culture, his example as a writer of fiction, and his demonstration that the truths of the faith could be expressed in lively prose all contributed to the immeasurable boost that Lewis provided to evangelicals on this side of the water.

The glue uniting the different strands of evangelical intellectual renewal came in several forms. Besides educational exchange carried on by private parties, notable individuals, projects, and institutions also made a contribution. The American evangelist, Billy Graham, was a contact point of nearly universal recognition. What he did on a large scale through popular evangelism to establish networks of evangelical interest was similar to the work that British missioners to the universities, like Martin Lloyd-Jones or John Stott, accomplished among more strictly academic groups. Cooperative publishing ventures, like the *New Bible Commentary* and the *New Bible Dictionary* from British InterVarsity, Henry's work at *Christianity Today*, and several different projects at Eerdmans, drew evangelical scholars from both sides of the Atlantic into a common labor. Eventually, other institutions, like the American InterVarsity Christian Fellowship or the Lausanne Committee for World Evangelization, became arenas that strengthened cross-cultural evangelical ties.

The result has been the establishment of an evangelical intellectual network with certain well-fixed reference points in the United States, Great Britain, and Canada, as well as other parts of the world. The extended connections of British InterVarsity, the insights of Dutch Reformed confessionalists, the common valuing of the classical Protestant heritage, and an ingrained respect for an even broader range of historic Christian expressions have all shaped the parts of this coalition.

The new leaders of a more intellectually aggressive evangelicalism also took in hand the revitalization of institutions. Already in the 1930s, a few colleges with evangelical convictions were beginning to emerge from the trauma of Fundamentalist separation. Even more significant was progress in advanced study. During the 1940s, Fuller Theological Seminary joined Westminster as a professional school dedicated not only to the preparation of ministers but also to the prosecution of research. Before another two decades had passed, other seminaries—Bethel, Asbury, Gordon-Conwell, Trinity, and several of the Southern Baptist, Adventist, and Church of Christ schools—were also stressing academic thoroughness in a refreshing way. If the scholarly reinvigoration that resulted was most visible for work in biblical studies, these evangelicals testified to a much more serious engagement of the mind through their thorough academic preparation and dedicated approach to learning. After World War II evangelicals also formed a series of academic associations, some focusing on biblical and theological subjects, but others also for the increased numbers of professionals in philosophy, history, literature, sociology, economics, and the other academic disciplines.

In sum, the intellectual situation for evangelicals since the era of the Fundamentalist-Modernist controversy is much improved. Striking gains have been made. The need for Christian thinking has been recognized. And significant steps have been taken toward promoting a Christian mind, not only in the field of theology but also for other aspects of existence. At the same time, we must be careful not to congratulate ourselves too much. Our recent gains have been modest. The general impact of Christian thinking on the *Christians* of our country, much less the nation's academic culture, is slight. Evangelicals of several types have begun to do what needs to be done if we would develop a Christian mind, or at least we have begun to talk about what would need to be done for such a mind to develop. But there is a long, long way to go. The distance still to be traveled comes into clearer focus if we stop to think about the state of theology among evangelicals and if we examine the impact that evangelicals have made to date on the institutions that exert the most intellectual influence upon our everyday lives.

Recognizing Current Limitations

Despite a good bit of respectable recent work in theology, it would be an exaggeration to say that evangelical theology is now a flourishing intellectual enterprise. This area, which touches evangelical self-definition so directly, has been the focus of much energy; but it has also suffered from a number of the more general circumstances affecting evangelical life. Evangelicalism still shows the effects of decades of controversy, first with liberal Christians and the secular academy over the Bible's inspiration, but also with other theologically conservative believers over the exact character of biblical authority. In addition, the use by evangelicals of the church's rich heritage has been hampered by the American fixation upon the present. The notion that Christians from prior generations could sharpen the minds of believers in our own day is all too rare among evangelicals. Evangelical engagement with the intellectual world of the late twentieth century is also sporadic in a way that impedes theology. Modern developments in philosophy, the history and philosophy of science, the social sciences, and even in theology from non-evangelical sources are all important for establishing the conceptual conventions of our day. Yet evangelicals all too regularly pass by such matters as if they were irrelevant to the theological task.

To be sure, we evangelicals enjoy some good work in theology. Some comes from philosophers, social scientists, and literary scholars who write theologically about their specialties. Some also comes from our theological synthesizers who have competently refurbished older theological formulas for contemporary purposes. Much of this work is unquestionably helpful. What is often lacking, however, is intellectual creativity and literary force. All too often our theology lacks the benefit from prolonged reading in the history of Christian doctrine and meaningful appreciation of modern intellectual developments. If such limitations prevail among the better products of contemporary evangelical theology, things are much worse at the pedestrian level where wild eschatological speculation, wooden prooftexting, and anti-intellectual sermonizing regularly are passed off for serious theology. It says a great deal for modern evangelicals that nineteenth-century textbooks by Charles Hodge, A. H. Strong, and one or two others still are among the most ambitious and comprehensive evangelical works of systematic theology in print. It is also a revealing sign of the times that the most arresting theological books read widely by American evangelicals are probably still occasional works by Britons like Lewis or G. K. Chesterton.

The pursuit of intellectual life seems to have its special difficulties at evangelical seminaries, institutions that, on the whole, have shown a great deal of maturity in recent decades. Here the problem is one of diffused energies. At evangelical seminaries some first-rank intellectuals devote a disproportionate share of their energies to itinerant preaching and the writing of popular books. Such assignments are legitimate, yet they make it very difficult for these scholars to pursue the life of the mind as an avenue of Christian service to the academic community. As a consequence, the realm of first order thinking, which exerts such a tremendous indirect influence on modern life, remains largely untouched by evangelical insight.

But our intellectual limitations today extend also well beyond the seminaries. Christian colleges, like Wheaton College where I teach, have made rapid progress in the postwar years, but the distance remaining before such places become first-rate reservoirs of thought is still great. A recent paper by the Princeton sociologist Robert Wuthnow, who is quite sympathetic to evangelical convictions, spotlighted some of the problems of these evangelical colleges. Wuthnow pointed out that the deep structures of modern intellectual life are shaped largely by the works of non- or anti-Christians. Theorists like Marx, Weber, Durkheim, and Freud established the modern intellectual conventions of the academy. Their legacy, for good and for ill, provides the framework in which Christians pursue their advanced studies. But it is more than just the framework of modern intellectual life that constricts the evangelical life of the mind. It is also the widely varying distribution of academic resources. A handful of national research universities act as gatekeepers, intellectual and physical, for most of the learned professions. If evangelicals are to be academically certified, they must pass through those gates. But then, if they would mount convincing efforts to change the academic landscape, they must do so with resources that cannot begin to compare with those enjoyed by the major research universities. As Wuthnow put it, "those who would wish to see a distinctively Evangelical scholarly orientation advanced are at a tremendous competitive disadvantage. To pit even the strong Evangelical aspirations of a Wheaton College or a Calvin College, or the massive fund-raising network of a Liberty University, against the multi-billion dollar endowments of a Princeton or a Harvard reveals the vast extent of this deficit in resources."

In words even more chilling than Wuthnow's, Charles Malik spoke in 1980 of the nature of the challenge to Christians who take to heart the seriousness of the intellectual life. As Malik put it, "At the heart of all the problems facing Western civilization—the general nervousness and restlessness, the dearth of grace and beauty and quiet and peace of soul, the manifold blemishes and perversions of personal character; problems of the family and of social relations in general, problems of economics and politics, problems of the media, problems affecting the school itself and the church itself, problems in the international order—at the heart of the crisis in Western civilization lies the state of the mind and the spirit of the universities." Malik suggested that since the dilemmas of modern life are intellectual dilemmas, dilemmas of the sort the universities exist to explore, it is important for Christians to realize the magnitude of their intellectual task. As he put it, "The problem is not only to win souls but to save minds. If you win the whole world and lose the mind of the world, you will soon discover that you have not won the world. Indeed it may turn out that you have actually lost the world."

But then Malik turned to look at the contribution of evangelicals. He was not unappreciative of the good work evangelicals have been doing since World War II, but his words described the nature of our intellectual challenge with uncommon force: "the greatest danger besetting American Evangelical Christianity is the danger of anti-intellectualism. The mind as to its greatest and deepest riches is not cared for enough. This cannot take place apart from profound immersion for a period of years in the history of thought and the spirit. People are in a hurry to get out of the university and start earning money or serving the church or preaching the gospel. They have no idea of the infinite value of spending years of leisure in conversing with the greatest minds and souls of the past, and thereby ripening and sharpening and enlarging their powers of thinking. The result is that the arena of creative thinking is abdicated and vacated to the enemy. Who among the Evangelicals can stand up to the great secular or naturalistic or atheistic scholars on their own terms of scholarship and research? Who among the Evangelical scholars is quoted as a normative source by the greatest secular authorities on history or philosophy or psychology or sociology or politics? Does your mode of thinking have the slightest chance of becoming the dominant mode of thinking in the great universities of Europe and America which stamp your entire civilization with their own spirit and ideas?

"It will take a different spirit altogether to overcome this great danger of anti-intellectualism. . . . Even if you start now on a crash program in this and other domains, it will be a century at least before you catch up with the Harvards and Tübingens and the Sorbonnes, and think of where these universities will be then! For the sake of greater effectiveness in witnessing to Jesus Christ himself, as well as for their own sakes, the Evangelicals cannot afford to keep on living on the periphery of responsible intellectual existence."

If Malik's words are discouraging about the task that remains in elite culture, think what could be said about evangelical influence in the popular media that is just as influential in shaping our thinking, that also constructs the mind with which we live in the world. Have we as evangelicals even made a start in providing intellectual shape to the world of popular culture and the popular media? And what are the results if we let Madison Avenue, Hollywood, ESPN, and the publishers of *USA Today* shape the contours of our minds? If anything, such questions reveal a more profoundly disturbing intellectual situation than the situation created by the elite learned culture of the universities.

Posing Questions about the Future

In conclusion, let me repeat as clearly as possible why it is important for evangelicals to be concerned about such questions of the intellect. What difference does it make if we pursue the life of the mind or if we do not? What is at stake in the development of an evangelical mind? At least three things, it seems to me, are at stake. They may be framed as questions.

First is a question with great practical implications. Who will be our tutors, the ones who teach us and our children about life? The institutions of learned culture and the great engine of the American mass media are the two prime contenders for this task in our world. The universities nourish the thinkers who propose grand paradigms through which we examine the world. The producers of MTV, Johnny Carson, Steven Spielberg, and the movers and shakers of Hollywood provide a never-ending series of flashy stimulants that also have a profound intellectual affect. Each of us is developing a mind with which we reason about all areas of life—political allegiance as well as Christian conversion, the meaning of money as well as the meaning of the Bible, the effects of democracy as well as the effects of sin. Who will teach us how to reason about these matters? Who will be our guides pointing us to truth and light? If we evangelicals do not take seriously the larger world of the intellect, we say, in effect, that we want our minds to be shaped by the conventions of our modern universities and the assumptions of Madison Avenue, instead of by God and the servants of God.

A second question moves beyond the practical to the spiritual. It is the question of how we will live in the world. But this too is an intensely intellectual question. How we live in the world depends in large measure on how we think about the world. For Christians it is all too easy simply to join the herd, simply to think that life exists as a series of opportunities for pleasure, self-expression, and the increase of comfort. But it is also possible as Christians to take the other extreme, to think that the world through which we move is just an unreal shadow preparing the way for our home beyond the skies. Such thinking is not altogether wrong. The Christian belief in eternity is one of the most important of our convictions. At the same time, not to think about the ways in which life in this world can be lived because of God, and for God, is to cheapen and neglect a whole realm of existence. But to accept this life as a gift from God, to live as though a deeper understanding of existence is a deeper understanding of God, requires dedicated and persistent thought, even as it requires dedicated and persistent spiritual vitality.

Again, Blamires has put very well the intellectual issue involved in living our lives to the glory of God. "The question is, will the Christians of the next fifty years, over against a strengthened secularism, deepen and clarify their Christian commitment in a withdrawn cultivation of personal morality and spirituality . . . ? Or will the Christians of the next fifty years deepen and clarify their Christian commitment at the intellectual and social levels too, meeting and challenging not only secularism's assault upon personal morality and the life of the soul, but also secularism's truncated and perverted view of the meaning of life and the purpose of the social order?" To mount that challenge to the meaning of life and the purpose of the social order means to develop a Christian mind.

Finally, and ultimately, the question of Christian thinking is a spiritual question. What sort of God will we worship? With this question we return again to the most important matter concerning a Christian mind. The search for a Christian perspective on life—on our families, our economies, our leisure activities, our sports, our attitudes pertaining to the body and to health care, our reactions to novels and paintings, as well as our churches and our specifically Christian activities—is not just an academic exercise. The search for a Christian mind is rather an effort to take seriously the sovereignty of God over the world he created, the lordship of Christ over the world he died to redeem, and the power of the Holy Spirit over the world he sustains each and every moment. From this perspective the search for an evangelical mind takes on ultimate significance, because the search for an evangelical mind is not, in the end, a search for mind, but a search for God.

Suggestions for Further Reading

Hatch, Nathan O. "Evangelical Colleges and the Challenge of Christian Thinking." *The Reformed Journal* (September 1985): 10–18.

Hatch explains why the activistic, democratic, and person-ality-centered character of American evangelicalism has left the movement ill-equipped to mount and sustain meaningful ventures in higher education.

Holmes, Arthur F. *All Truth Is God's Truth* (Grand Rapids: Eer-dmans, 1977); *The Idea of a Christian College* (Grand Rapids: Eerdmans, 1987); ed., *The Making of a Christian Mind: A Christian World View and the Academic Enterprise* (Downers Grove, Ill.: InterVarsity, 1985).

Holmes, a philosopher at Wheaton College in Illinois, has been a leader in articulating a rationale for higher educa-tion from the Christian standpoint. *All Truth Is God's Truth* uses traditional evangelical categories of sin, revela-tion, and Christology to defend the academic enterprise against anti-intellectualism. *The Idea of a Christian College* presents a confessional evangelical setting as an ideal place to study the liberal arts. In *The Making of a Christian Mind* Holmes is joined by four of his Wheaton colleagues to suggest how Christian thinking can take place within the disciplines and be an influence upon them.

Malik, Charles. *A Christian Critique of the University* (Downers Grove, Ill.: InterVarsity, 1982).

Malik, a former leader of the United Nations and an Ortho-dox Christian, asks what a Christian stance toward univer-sity education should be, in light of the fact that the most important critic of the Western universities "in the final analysis is Jesus Christ himself."

Marsden, George. *The Soul of the American University* (New York: Oxford University Press, 1994).

Marsden surveys the history of America's oldest universities, founded as Protestant institutions committed to distinctively Christian higher education, and argues that they have become secular institutions where the Christian religion is marginalized and undervalued.

Noll, Mark A. *The Scandal of the Evangelical Mind* (Grand Rapids: Eerdmans, 1994).

The germinal ideas found in the chapter published for this anthology came to full blossom in this book. Noll writes that "the scandal of the evangelical mind is that there is not much of an evangelical mind." This critical yet constructive book explains the decline of American evangelical scholarship and seeks to find within evangelicalism resources to counteract the decay that has been taking place.

Wuthnow, Robert. *The Struggle for America's Soul: Evangelicals, Liberals, and Secularism* (Grand Rapids: Eerdmans, 1989).

Wuthnow discusses four fundamental aspects of our current secular culture: civil privatism, the media, the preeminence of science, and academia. He also examines the evangelical responses to the marginalization of Christianity in the university and presses for re-engagement and re-entry.

Yandell, Keith E., ed. "A New Agenda for Evangelical Thought." *Christian Scholars Review* 17 (June 1988): 341–488.

This special issue was devoted to a series of essays on evangelical scholarly participation in the academic disciplines: Mary Stewart Van Leeuwen on psychology, Patricia Ward and David Jeffrey on literature, Nicholas Wolterstorff on the arts, Carl F. H. Henry on Christian scholarship in a fallen world, George Marsden on the general state of evangelical Christian scholarship, and other scholars on additional topics.

2

The Evangelical Agenda

Bruce Shelley

The day of the professional minister is over. The day of the missionary pastor has come. This is the arresting conclusion of Kennon Callahan in his book, *Effective Church Leadership*. "Some may wonder," says Callahan, "if this startling bold prophecy will come true. I can assure you, that it will not come true in the future because it has already happened. The professional minister movement ended quietly, suitably, and decently enough a few years ago as professional ministers experienced a gridlock of meetings, desks stacked with papers, calendars filled with appointments, and declining worship attendance in their churches. There was no climactic event, no dramatic conclusion. The professional minister movement, born in the church culture of the late 1940s, simply ceased to be functional on the mission field of the 1980s."

Callahan has a way of getting your attention. His implicit suggestion that seminary education may be next to worthless in America's neo-pagan culture—as well as the prospects of unemployment for faculty members—makes one sit up and take thought. At least I did. Will seminaries survive? Callahan's intent, of course, is not to describe the actual passing of the professional ministry. He is announcing its irrelevance for effective ministry in a secular society. That is something quite different. He is underscoring today's need for men and women whose vision for ministry is focused on people outside the church rather than those inside.

Callahan's words are especially useful in setting a tone for my topic, the evangelical agenda. Any historian worth his contract would not touch such a topic, even with a student assistant. Scholars are not generally into agendas. For a preacher, however, it is a temptation akin to the call to a larger church. The term *agenda* itself is not the problem. After all, agendas are simply lists of things to be done. This topic, the evangelical agenda, however, fills our heads with more questions than answers. Which evangelical agenda, I first asked myself; is there only one? Has not Jerry Falwell already published, in *Listen, America,* his agenda for the Christian Right? Has not the evangelical counterculture begun to revive models from the Hutterite *bruderhofs?* The point is, it would appear, there does not seem to be a single, unified agenda available for evangelicals today. Consequently, what I present to you must be my understanding of the task before us—one that I hope some of you will share with me.

Let me follow Callahan's lead, then, by a case study in leadership that I discovered two years ago in Ogden, Utah. Perhaps you ought to consider this a report from the hinterland or a vignette from Bill Moyers's *The Life of the Mind.* It is the story of a church you have probably never seen and a pastor you have probably never met. I accepted an invitation to be an adult teacher for the family Vacation Bible School at Washington Heights Church in Ogden, Utah. To be honest, I accepted the invitation in part out of respect for two of our graduates who were serving in the church. I was rewarded that week, however, with material for my courses and for reflection upon the evangelical agenda far beyond my wildest hopes.

Washington Heights Church was established in 1955 during the Eisenhower years. Hundreds and perhaps thousands of churches were established in the mid-1950s. For twenty-eight years in the Salt Lake Valley, as was true in many other regions, Washington Heights had struggled to maintain an attendance of approximately 130. Then came 1983 and a remarkable turnaround—much like some I have heard of in New England. Today Washington Heights Church draws more than 600 people to its Sunday morning worship, making it one of the largest evangelical churches in the greater Salt Lake area.

What produced this remarkable turnaround? In the shadows of the everlasting hills, as the Mormons like to say, Washington Heights Church shifted from a professional ministry, maintaining all the regular services for all the regular worshipers, to a missionary ministry, reaching out to religious seekers in a foreign culture. During that week in Ogden I had noon and evening meals with members in modest mobile homes; I had lunches in city parks; I had dinners in stylishly-appointed residences. I brainstormed for three hours with the church staff and I listened to scores of people as they told me about the changes in their personal lives and the life of their church. There in Ogden, Utah, I began to see an evangelical agenda unfolding.

Identifying Our Operating Assumptions

Before turning to that agenda, however, I would like to identify a few of my operating assumptions. My first assumption is this: we are living in a culturally diverse, pluralistic America. This is revealed to us in a thousand ways,

I suppose, but one of the more fascinating is in a recent book by Michael J. Weis, *The Clustering of America,* in which he sketches the portraits of forty American life-styles based, if you can believe it, upon postal service zip codes.

My second assumption is this: that America experienced a cultural revolution in the 1960s. Evangelical Christians were at that time added to the list of American minorities. Ideals within the biblical and secular strands of American culture drifted farther and farther apart. Americans could no longer claim to share the same code of ethics, the same religious faith, the same idea of patriotism, or the same image of the American dream. The American "new class," which is Peter Berger's word for the academic, entertainment, and media elite in America, came to view these changes as important advances in human freedom and dignity. The easing of divorce laws, the tolerance of new lifestyles, the legalization of abortion, and the end of artistic censorship were to be applauded. To conservative Americans, the same decades were judged to be marked by moral decadence, national decline, and a social revolution that can be compared, as Charles Colson and others have done, to the barbarian overthrow of the Christian Roman Empire.

Many Christians are screaming for reform. But where does reform begin? Some believers are so angry over abortions on demand and prejudice against Christians in the public schools that they are calling for nothing less than a reconstruction of the American republic on the explicit laws of God. They challenge the whole idea of the enlightened progressive creed that undergirds secular liberalism. The evangelicals I met in Utah, however, were not screaming. They know that they are a religious minority. Now they are asking what this fact means for their families and for their church.

My third assumption is that the agenda of modern secular liberalism is economic progress, universal liberation, and expressive individualism. Such secular liberalism is not a live option for evangelicals. Most, I suspect, would consider this view of life and reality largely bankrupt. The secular dream claims that every step forward in the intellectual, social, and political fields is part of a movement toward a universal liberation. Minorities are being liberated from political oppressors; labor from enslavement to capitalists; women from servitude to men; children from the tyranny of parents; citizens from the constraints of poverty; homosexuals from the laws against perversion; couples from the prison of lifelong marriage; and monkeys from ruthless researchers. The myth stresses what could be called an escalating emancipation, since life seems to produce an endless stream of tyrants. As a result, the business of dismantling restrictions from the past must go on indefinitely. The fact that some of these liberations are highly desirable has encouraged the notion that all of them must be. This gospel of human progress is a Christian heresy because it rests on the assumption that humankind has progressed, not by the discipline of the ego, but by feeding the insatiable appetite within every one of us. Evangelicals, along with many other Christians, consider such a view of reality self-defeating, a dead-end street.

My fourth assumption is that evangelicals in pluralistic America have come to reflect, at least to some degree, the cultural spectrum of the country. I think you must enter ministry today with the pluralistic view of the field of ministry. By the cultural spectrum I mean the cultural left, the cultural center, and the cultural right. The strength of American evangelicals is on the right, where self-denial lives on in the reverence for traditional families, the American flag, and a full day's work. Evangelical churches in the suburbs, however, give clear evidence of the influence of the success-oriented center of American cultural life. Most evangelical schools reflect many of the values of the center and some of the values of the left.

Finally, in discussing an evangelical agenda, I am assuming that "evangelical" means to you what it means to me, namely, that company of American Christians committed to the authority of the Bible, the centrality of a personal experience of the grace of God and the responsibility of making this good news known to those outside the household of faith.

Recovering Community

Now, with that ground cleared, let me turn to the planting of a few seeds of thought regarding a possible agenda for America's evangelicals. At the top of the list, in my limited judgment, is a recovery of a lost experience. The experience of which I speak is the discovery of church as a vital community. Community tops the list because the Bible so clearly asserts the centrality of *koinonia*, the common life in the body of Christ. Community also tops the list because our contemporaries, both inside and outside the church, reveal so many signs of spiritual loneliness.

Modernity, with its stress on individual rights and an economy based on personal choice, has almost completely undermined the foundation of community life at almost every level—in our small towns, in our families, in our churches, and in our business corporations. Governments at all levels reveal serious stress fractures from the impact of a gospel of self-expression. I am thinking in particular of a book titled *The Cultural Contradiction of Capitalism.* In a democracy like ours, this book claims, society exists mainly to support the expressions of individuality. That is what democracy is about, namely, the support of the expressions of individuality. We assume that if we are free enough to choose whatever we want—Nike, Converse, or Reebok, for example—we can postpone forever the question of what "needs" are worth having and on what basis we ought to make those choices.

The good life becomes a supermarket of desires. What we call freedom often becomes a form of inward tyranny. As we go about fulfilling our needs and asserting our rights we live like strangers to one another. The church, for its part, often becomes one more drive-up consumer-oriented organization. We miss completely the biblical emphasis of salvation as a process of spiritual maturity within the church, the community of God.

In recent years, influential sociologists have revealed the damaging effects of our gospel of self-expression. We are trying to make it without our "communities of memories." These communities of memories include our families and churches, with their living traditions. We hear this theme like a haunting melody running through that very popular and widely read book, *Habits of the Heart*. "The question," Bellah and his associates write, "is whether an individualism in which the self has become the main form of reality can really be sustained. This quest for purely private fulfillment is illusory. It often ends in emptiness. One cannot live a rich, private life in a state of siege, mistrusting all strangers and turning one's home into an armed camp. Our problems today are not just political; they are moral and have to do with the meaning of life. We are beginning to see that our common life requires more than an exclusive concern for material accumulation."

Happily, some theologians have offered a Christian alternative to the gospel of self-expression. Among these articulate advocates of life in community are John Howard Yoder, Stanley Hauerwas, and William Willimon. They argue that we need to dismiss all ideas of the church as merely a useful supportive institution and ministers as primarily members of a helping profession. The church has its own reason for being and its own mandate for ministry. It is not commissioned by the powers of the world. To make their point clear, they distinguish three basic types of churches: the activist church, the conversionist church, and the confessing church.

The activist church, illustrated primarily by many within the mainline denominations, is more concerned with the building of a better society than it is with the vitality of the church. It calls upon its members to seek God at work and to get behind the movements for social change. Christians must join in movements for justice wherever they might find them. The problem with this view of the church, however, is its practice of operating without any clear biblical truth whereby to judge history and its own best efforts within that history. As a result, its politics are usually a sort of religiously glorified liberalism.

The conversionist church argues that no amount of tinkering with the structures of society will overcome the effects of human sin. The promises of secular optimism are therefore false, because they attempt to bypass the biblical call to admit personal guilt and to experience reconciliation with God and neighbor. The conversionist church, therefore, shifts from the sphere of political action without to the condition of the soul within, from society to the individual.

The confessing church is not a generic blend of the other two; rather, it is much more akin to a radical alternative, rejecting both the secularism of the activists and the individualism of the conversionists. The confessing church finds its primary task neither in the reordering of society nor in the personal transformation of individuals, but in the congregation's commitment to follow Christ in all things. It begins with the spiritual vitality of the community. The confessing church, like the conversionist church, calls people to conversion, to be sure, but it considers conversion to be a lifelong process of being ingrafted into a new people, the countercultural structure called the church. Its aim is to influence the world by being something the world is not, and can never be—it aims to be the visible church, the community in which people are faithful to their promises, in which they love their enemies, tell the truth, honor the poor, suffer for righteousness, and thereby testify to the power of God.

Allow me to put this first item on the agenda in specific terms. In the summer of 1983, morale was so low at Washington Heights Church that the staff decided for the first time in years they would have no summer Bible school. No one seemed to care. In November of that same year, however, Les and Beulah MaGee arrived in Ogden to assume leadership of this struggling church. They had been missionaries in Brazil and Portugal for twenty-three years and saw the potential for a family Vacation Bible School, especially in Utah. So, in June of 1984, the church resurrected the Bible School and, to their amazement, some 200 attended. People were so enthusiastic about the family experience, in fact, that a year later they agreed to scrap the anemic midweek activities for a Wednesday night family program, beginning with a dinner. The first Wednesday on which the new program was to be launched, 200 people turned out for the meal, the Bible study, the children's activity, and relaxed conversation. It was a turning point in the growth of that church. Family night program now regularly attracts more than 400 people. This year's family Vacation Bible School had 640 in attendance throughout that week.

What caused the change, you might ask? The answer is community. In a culture where family values are revered, this evangelical church offers a weekly experience in vital community. In the business and educational climate of the area, evangelical Christians have a dozen reminders every week that they are, in fact, a minority. Those of you who know Utah will understand what I am saying. Perhaps we could translate it to another religious culture and make comparisons with New England. Not surprisingly, these people find family night at their church a refreshing and invigorating experience with, as they say, "our own people." That can be said in the wrong way, of course, but if it is stressing the quality of the community, it can also be said in the right way. I do not know how this church as a distinct, divine community strikes you, but it impresses me that it is a biblical point aimed appropriately at the heart of American individualism and especially its success-oriented culture. If evangelicals are now a cultural minority, then they must begin to think and minister as a vital community, stripped of all the traditional privileges and expectations of cultural dominance that it once enjoyed.

Recovering the Conviction of an Evangelistic Mission

This vision of the confessing church, however, needs to be supplemented, in my judgment, by a second item on the agenda. Evangelical Christians must renew their conviction that the church is also on a mission from God. The Yoder/Hauerwas/Willimon vision needs the vigor of the American revival tradition—not its individualism, mind you, but its sense of mission to the American society. Countercultural movements, however, do not have an impressive track record for evangelism and church growth. That fact makes most evangelicals uneasy. We need reminders of the excesses of revivalism, to be sure. So many visions of "Christ for America" campaigns have been corrupted by serious compromises with American culture. From the Puritan myth of a New Israel and the Anglo-Saxon superiority of the manifest destiny, to the health-and-wealth gospel of recent televangelists, compromises have all too often been made with American culture.

But is there not also a danger on the other side? Have not confessing minorities shown a marked tendency to neglect the Bible's evangelistic mandate? By shunning relevance, have they not often confessed the truth to fewer and fewer Christians? Do we believe that the traditional Christian mission to America has been rescinded? Most evangelicals now seem to settle for winning a few individual souls here and there and gathering them into some exclusive little congregation. On the contrary, evangelism remains a mandate; so does the preservation of the traditional family, the multiplication of spiritually vibrant congregations, Christian education for the young and newly converted, and Christian ministries of compassion in the public realm. These all remain priorities for Christians in America. Only now, in the presence of "the barbarians," if I might again borrow Colson's term, these ministries must be conducted as strategies of a minority, not efforts of the party of power.

Allow me one little incident during my week in Utah to illustrate this point. When I arrived in the church building to preach on Sunday morning, I had prayer with the other worship leaders and walked to the worship center with Pastor MaGee. In the forty or so steps that we took toward the swinging doors, we had just enough time for him to turn to me and say, "I hope you're not planning any put-downs of our neighbors this morning." I knew instantly what he meant, and I assured him that I never made a practice of criticizing other faiths. It was a relatively minor exchange, but the reason for recalling it is the pastor's attitude. He expected seekers to be there and he knew the importance of a winsome experience within the Christian community. He thought as a missionary pastor should think.

Developing Transformational Leaders

As a third item on the agenda, let me suggest that evangelical seminaries must purpose to develop men and women who are more than professionals (not less, of course, but certainly more than professionals)—men and women who are transformational leaders. Changing times, it seems, bring new meanings to ministry. The understanding of a minister as a professional developed between the 1920s and the 1950s and tended to dominate congregational life for about a half-century. The professional leader worked within the church. He or she was the institutional figure. He or she was committed to keeping people happy and the program on schedule. Our times, however, demand something more. We need missionary pastors or, as some would say, transformational leaders. One cannot travel for many months in evangelical circles without detecting the frustrations of the ministry. Ministers in local churches, in particular, face unprecedented expectations. People want their pastors to be informed, articulate, and charismatic. They expect them to be as attractive and well-groomed as is the anchorman on the television news, yet as gentle and caring as their grandfather—and available for every crisis they face. Through all the real and unreal expectations there are also the relentless weekly sermons, budgets, and committee meetings.

The Southern Baptist Convention, our nation's largest Protestant denomination, reports that 116 pastors per month are terminated by their churches, an increase of 31 percent since 1984. Serving without the benefit of a job description and with no clear sense of purpose, other than the meeting of people's needs, many young pastors today find no way to limit what people expect or ask of them. Without a clear vision of either biblical community or biblical mission, too many pastors try to do everything and be everything for everybody. The most conscientious of them become empty and exhausted casualties. Without a vision the people and their leaders perish.

Many of you will detect that I am pressing the distinction between transactional and transformational leadership. Lyle Schaller, perhaps the best-known analyst of church life in America today, sharpened the difference in the two types when he wrote, "The majority of ministers appear to accept the role of a transactional leader and coach to enable focus on people in general and on individuals in particular. This is appropriate and highly popular in smaller congregations, who love gregarious, articulate, person-centered, extroverted and caring transactional leadership. By contrast, the transformational leader is driven by a vision of a new tomorrow, wins supporters and followers of that vision and transforms the congregation. The change from growing older and smaller to growing younger and larger, represents radical change, discontinuity; and it requires a new set of priorities. It is a transformation."

To illustrate these two types, I go back to Ogden, our case study, and Washington Heights Church. Prior to 1983 and the arrival of Pastor MaGee, the leadership of that church was transactional. The focus was within the congregation. The leaders worked hard to care for the one hundred or so saints, but they seemed to lack the vision, the training, and the gifts for reaching people beyond the church family. The minister was helpful to the insiders, but it was ministry in the maintenance mode. Pastor MaGee brought not only his missionary experience, but

also his low-key (and it is genuinely low-key) transformational leadership. Leadership is no longer the mystery it
once was for those of us in seminary education. We now
know, thanks to more than 260 studies on leadership, that
it has basic components. Leadership starts with vision. A
leader's vision is an image of a possible and desirable future for the church or parachurch ministry. It serves as a
bridge from the present conditions to the future possibilities in ministry. When a transformational leader can successfully communicate this image of the future to the
members of the church, people at all levels are more likely
to find their niche and their role in the ministry of the
church. If there is a genius in leadership, it is the ability to
assemble out of all the varieties of images, clues, and op-
tions, a clear vision of the future that people can readily
share and instinctively desire.

Transformational leaders always add to vision their effective communication. This is what effective football
coaches bring to a losing team. They have the ability to re-
store confidence by communicating a new enthusiasm for
winning and a commitment in players to pay the price for
victories. All of us have been observers of some athletic
team that has been turned around simply by new leadership. In order to do this within a church, transformational
leaders must change what students of this discipline call
the congregation's social architecture. The term stands
for the norms and the values that shape the behavior of
people within the church. Human nature being what it is,
we can always expect people to resist change. The transformational leader, however, has the power to gain a commitment to the new vision by projecting the benefits of the
vision clearly and frequently.

Finally, the effective leader sustains both the vision
and the communication by the trust of the members.
People need to know what the church is about and what

it is trying to do. It is the business of leaders to tell them, demonstrating week after week their competence in the skills of ministry. Trust gained becomes trust guarded, so leaders must be both consistent in their pursuit of moral principle and open to the ideas and challenges of others. There is an openness about transformational leaders.

The bottom line is that leadership is a skill that can be learned and developed; it is not something only a few possess from birth. What counts is a vision clearly communicated to a church or a ministry empowered by the leader to reach a common goal. These marks of transformational leadership—vision, communication, and trust—are precisely what I found at Washington Heights Church. When I met with the church staff to discuss the church, its culture, and the strategies for growth, I proposed at one point that they might want to capitalize on their growth by planting new congregations. For the first time in our extended discussions, I sensed suddenly the pastor's resistance. "That's not for us," he said. "I spent years in Brazil helping to plant small, obscure congregations with no cultural impact. We don't want that here. Evangelicals will get people's attention in this area only by size and visibility. In this culture, size is itself a witness." That is vision! Transformational leaders, as Schaller says, must then move on to win support and gain followers of the vision.

Within two years of Pastor MaGee's coming, Washington Heights faced the challenge of building a new fellowship hall. Older members within the congregation supported a building just big enough to meet the then-existing need as they saw it. But Pastor MaGee and his staff were able to convince the church to plan for growth and to double the size of the building. It was done and growth came. In a few years, the plan for growth reached much further. As the people came to trust their leaders, the church secured new property—interestingly, it was a gravel pit, but they got it for a reasonable price. A gravel pit! But more importantly, that gravel pit was located on a major thoroughfare, a national highway. There they constructed an attractive complex of buildings, including a gymnasium for their popular family nights. The architect for the project was himself converted during the long months of building, impressed in part by the leaders of the church and their integrity in dealing with him. When the building was dedicated, the leaders made a point of welcoming Mormons to see what an evangelical church looks like from the inside out. The idea was not a new one; the same courtesy is extended to non-Mormons for days just before a Mormon temple is dedicated. My point is simple: evangelicals need more transformational leaders like Pastor MaGee—men and women with the gifts and training to form and cultivate Christian communities and who reach out in loving concern to people in America's changing landscape.

Yet, we are left with a haunting question: Can seminaries provide those leaders? In his recent book, *U.S. Lifestyles in Mainline Churches*, Tex Sample, himself a seminary professor, argues that seminary training makes people unfit to serve congregations on the cultural right. The more a theological school sees itself as committed to the graduate study of religion, the more likely this is to be true. University and seminary training is socially located in a very different place from the cultural right, and it approaches truth in a way that mystifies many local people. It usually takes five years for the average seminary graduate to get in touch with local people—if he or she lasts that long. If Sample is right—and having lived a few years in the rural South, I tend to agree with him—are we prepared to continue educating people for ministry within a rather small segment of the American population?

We have been discussing these items—community, mission, and leadership—for a year at the seminary in which I am privileged to teach and we have been asking, "Is it realistic to expect a seminary to prepare all of its students in this transformational way?" Our somewhat tentative conclusion is that it probably is not. Our traditional programs may continue to produce transactional leaders, yet at the very least we will need a special program alongside the professional structures that stresses commitment to Christian community, cultural awareness, and transformational leadership.

Mounted near my desk in my office is a colorful poster with a pithy caption. This poster is about fourteen by twenty inches in size. When a friend gave it to me a few years ago, I could not help but imagine that it portrays evangelical ministry today in a strikingly appropriate way. It shows a frog, about three feet in the air, stretched between two fragile reeds, clutching one reed with one front foot, and the other with its other three, in an obvious quandary. The caption reads: "Life is a predicament." In my culturally-conditioned judgment, this is a picture of the evangelical agenda today. It stresses the necessity of holding on while we reach out. The church of the near future and the leaders God provides for his people must distinguish a meaningful Christian engagement of American culture in its outreach ministry and a distinctive Christian alternative to American culture within its worshiping communities. It must break through the walls of isolation from American public life by the use of methods and ministries that make sense to secular-minded Americans. At the same time, the church must resist assimilation by that same American culture by maintaining a distinctively Christian worship, message, lifestyle, and leadership.

To conclude, let me echo the prayer of an eighteenth-century transformational leader who both transformed his culture and nurtured Christian communities. It was John Wesley who prayed, "Pardon, O gracious Jesus, what we have been. With your holy discipline correct what we are. Order by your providence what we shall be and in the end crown your own gifts. Amen."

Suggestions for Further Reading

Bellah, Robert N., Richard Madsen, William M. Sullivan, Ann Swidler, and Steven M. Tipton. *Habits of the Heart: Individualism and Commitment in American Life* (New York: Harper and Row, 1985).

This classic study concludes that Americans, largely confined to a vocabulary of individualism, have lost the language needed to make moral sense of their lives.

Callahan, Kennon L. *Twelve Keys to an Effective Church* (New York: Harper and Row, 1983); *Effective Church Leadership* (New York: Harper and Row, 1990).

Drawing on more than twenty years of experience, Callahan identifies the strengths and weaknesses found in today's churches and suggests how they can be used to produce more effective congregations.

Guinness, Os. *The American Hour: A Time of Reckoning and the Once and Future Role of the Faith* (New York: Free Press, 1993).

Guinness examines the ways in which the current crisis of cultural authority strikes at the heart of American identity. This crisis, he believes, has occurred because America's beliefs, traditions, and ideals—civic as well as religious—are losing their power to shape the private and public lives of countless Americans.

Hauerwas, Stanley, and William H. Willimon. *Resident Aliens: Life in the Christian Colony* (Nashville: Abingdon, 1989).

Hauerwas and Willimon explore the alien status of Christians in today's world and offer a compelling new vision of how the Christian church can regain its vitality, battle its malaise, reclaim its capacity to nourish souls, and stand firmly against the illusions, pretensions, and eroding values of today's world.

Hunter, James Davison. *American Evangelicalism: Conservative Religion and the Quandary of Modernity* (New Brunswick, N.J.: Rutgers University Press, 1983).

Hunter contends that evangelicalism has adapted to the constraints of modernity much more successfully than has its close relative, Fundamentalism. Exploring the reciprocal relationship between the church and culture, Hunter suggests that evangelicalism now looks virtually identical to the culture it sought to reform.

Marsden, George, ed. *Evangelicalism and Modern America* (Grand Rapids: Eerdmans, 1984).

Several prominent scholars seek to place evangelicalism within its larger cultural context.

Schaller, Lyle E. *Activating the Passive Church: Diagnosis and Treatment* (Nashville: Abingdon, 1981).

Schaller discusses the reasons for church passivity and formulates a method for helping congregations to emerge from the doldrums and to become more vibrant communities of faith.

Shelley, Bruce, and Marshall Shelley. *The Consumer Church: Can Evangelicals Win the World without Losing Their Souls?* (Downers Grove, Ill.: InterVarsity, 1992).

Suggesting that contemporary churches are often "pulled between faithfulness and effectiveness," the Shelleys offer guidance for what they call "ambidextrous ministry"—one that influences the world while remaining faithful to biblical teaching.

Wells, David F. *No Place for Truth, Or Whatever Happened to Evangelical Theology?* (Grand Rapids: Eerdmans, 1993); *God in the Wasteland: The Reality of Truth in a World of Fading Dreams* (Grand Rapids: Eerdmans, 1994).

In *No Place for Truth,* Wells describes modernity and analyzes its effects upon the church, the academy, and culture at large. In *God in the Wasteland,* he continues his analysis and suggests patterns for reform and rebirth within evangelicalism resulting in an appetite for truth that is currently lacking.

3

The Evangelical Contribution

Timothy L. Smith

One of the great remaining tasks for America's evangelical communities, I am convinced, is for them to explore more fully the multitude of religious traditions that have helped to shape their life and work. This task of identifying and relating the multiple strands of our larger movement is one that has long fascinated me and one that I would like for us to think about together.

Over the years, I have noticed that many of the evangelical communities that make up our wonderful fellowship here in America—and I need for accuracy to speak of them in the plural, although I dislike to do so—have a tendency to see themselves as the exclusive exemplars of the movement. As any historian knows, however, the evangelical mosaic is far more diverse and complex than any one of the groups that make it up. Indeed, the glory of evangelicalism can be found, in part, in its rich diversity. And its constituent parts have much to learn from one another.

Understanding Diverse Evangelical Traditions

I found myself recently in Pennsylvania Dutch country, driving slowly and lovingly across those beautiful spaces. Perhaps for the first time, I began to notice large numbers of Evangelical Congregational churches. Although I had on occasion spoken at their seminary at Myerstown, Pennsylvania, I had not previously noticed the strength and splendid condition of the many buildings put up by those who call themselves Evangelical Congregationalists. As many of you will already know, the background of that denomination is Wesleyan. They are part of the revival of Christian holiness that Wesleyan-oriented people brought to fruition in Lancaster County in the very heart of Pennsylvania Dutch country.

If you have occasion to visit Old Mannheim National Camp, located about ten miles from Lancaster, you will discover that those who planted this remarkable movement were a dissident group of Pennsylvania Germans. They and other dissenting groups before them had become Wesleyan or at least quasi-Wesleyan in their views and attitudes. As I thought about these people, I could not help but consider how appropriate it is that I should come from Pennsylvania to Massachusetts to address the theme of this session, the evangelical contribution, since (despite the differences) those Wesleyan evangelicals and you Reformed evangelicals are part of the same story. We belong to one another.

Indeed, it seems to me that when thinking about the history of evangelicalism in modern America one might just as appropriately begin in Pennsylvania as in New England. After all, when you stop to think about it, colonial Boston was much less like what America has become religiously than almost any place I know. Charleston, for example, was much closer to present patterns than was any community in the old Massachusetts Bay Colony. From the very beginning, Charleston was a varied community, pluralistic in nature, filled with Scotch-Irish, French Huguenots, Anglicans, and many others. Some of the early Baptists in America came directly to South Carolina from England. Among these were included, of all things, some of those General Baptists, who were less particular than some might wish them to have been. Particular Baptists, of course, believed in predestination. General Baptists, however, believed in what they call free grace. Some of the Yankee Baptists who went to the South to teach the settlers their Calvinistic Baptist ways were reconverted. Indeed, large numbers of Baptists in North Carolina and Virginia became General Baptists, that is, they came to believe in a general atonement—that everyone without exception could believe on the Lord Jesus Christ and be saved. We have almost forgotten about these remarkable people. Our primary interest is often centered in Philadelphia or Boston rather than in areas a bit farther south. Yet those people are also part of our family.

So I have set myself to studying as many of these groups as I can. I suppose it is because I am a Nazarene with a Wesleyan background that I tend to want more outsiders, those whose origins did not go back to New England, to join with me in celebrating the diverse rootage of modern American evangelicalism. What a magnificent kaleidoscope it is! When America was first settled, as you know, large numbers of Puritans came to Plymouth (1620) and then to Boston (1630). They established a great heritage, among other things, of a very strict Calvinism. Yet among them, right from the start, were Quakers and Baptists. It was a great day, in fact, when in 1660 the Baptists were able to build their own church in Boston.

The Quakers, likewise, scattered throughout the countryside from Maine to the Carolinas, began to grow in strength and power. Many of them became increasingly evangelical, in part as a result of the influence of those Quakers who stressed not only the inner light but also obedience to the outward Word. They came to believe in the kind of gospel that would look very familiar to most of us today. They were people who were saved by grace, and they spread that redemptive message across the country.

Many of you have heard about the Quakers in Oregon and George Fox College. George Fox is literally filled with Quakers. In chapel, they sing their hymns from a Nazarene hymnal. They are Wesleyan-holiness Quakers. There are other varieties, of course, but these march proudly under that banner. They believe in a general atonement and in the freedom of men and women to accept Jesus Christ and to be born again. These roots are planted just as deeply in colonial American soil as are those of the more Calvinistic groups.

Indeed, if you study the history of Quakers in Virginia, Ohio, Kansas, Oregon, Texas, and North Carolina, it is amazing to observe how this group of Christians has multiplied. These people too, like so many with whom we are more familiar, hire buses to hear Billy Graham preach, join enthusiastically in various parachurch organizations, and show up in the finest graduate schools around the country. They too are part of our fellowship.

Thanks to attractive preaching and the warm welcome of William Penn, great masses of poor Mennonites, Amish, Schwenkfelders, and others streamed in to Pennsylvania. There they discovered not only religious freedom but also abundant amounts of very rich land. As one drives along the back roads of Lancaster County, one sees the massive farms of those settlers and their offspring, one upon another. Here are some of the greatest farmers and farms in the world. And many are Pennsylvania German families who bought up as much land as they could from the Scotch-Irish and gave it to their sons. Their sons passed the farms along to their sons, and so on. And so it is that Lancaster County is today peopled by a great community of Mennonite and Amish people—people who were deeply evangelical long before the word was a household term. From the time of the Protestant Reformation of the sixteenth century they have believed and practiced scriptural religion—teaching and preaching the blessings of conversion and the importance of Christian mission.

I took a vacation once in Antigua. There I found Moravians and Methodists, most of whom were black. Their churches are beautiful, their worship is liturgical, and their theology is strict. Yet, they are as deeply evangelical as we are. Our great fellowship continues to grow.

We could also mention the Pietist movement of the seventeenth and eighteenth centuries in Europe. Many of America's evangelical Christians come from this great tradition. Indeed, the largest number of pastors in America's first Lutheran churches were Pietists. This was true for Mennonites as well. By the time of America's War for Independence, most Lutherans in the country were Pietists, located not only in Pennsylvania but in New York and the Shenandoah Valley as well. There, among those good Pennsylvania German people, was a community of evangelicals we have almost forgotten. The vision that they shared for the future of this country was just as great, as powerful, and as important in many ways as was that of the Congregationalists in New England.

As for the Methodists, we should remind ourselves that John Wesley and his Methodist preachers came to America quite late. John Wesley himself came to Georgia in the eighteenth century and eventually fled back to England where he remained until his death. Methodist preachers, products of the great Wesleyan revival that so profoundly marked English life and society, started to show up in the colonies on the eve of the American Revolution. Almost immediately, they began to preach to the Anglicans and others in Massachusetts and Connecticut, in New York and Pennsylvania. Large numbers of those traveling preachers also went to Virginia, and their ministries were remarkably effective. Operating as a society within the Church of England, they prayed and worked for gospel conversions and the outpouring of the grace of God upon the people of America.

Even Anglican ministers such as Devereux Jarratt became convinced Wesleyans. Having heard Wesley preach while he was in England and having read something of George Whitefield and John Fletcher, Jarratt came back to America to serve the Bath Parish in Dinwiddie County, Virginia. Hundreds of people in that vicinity were converted as a result of his powerful ministry. Vast crowds began to come to communion, and for years he remained the most powerful preacher in the Anglican church in Virginia, a community that to this day contains many evangelical believers.

There is an Anglican church near our home in Burke, Virginia. People there talk of going to healing services and of participating in various kinds of evangelical activities in relation to that parish. These too have become part of the fabric of America's great evangelical tradition. The study of American evangelicalism has often overlooked the importance of the Anglican tradition. Most English people were Anglicans—even those who were Calvinists. In fact, George Whitefield and John Wesley remained faithful Anglicans until they died. The Great Awakening itself involved Anglicans as well as Presbyterians, Congregationalists, and Baptists. When one thinks about the immense hold of Anglicanism on spiritual life in those early days, and one realizes that masses of Methodist converts were drawn from the Anglican church, one must conclude that there was something in the heritage of gospel preaching and teaching in Anglicanism that opened its followers in a special way to the gospel message.

All of this leads me to a rather surprising conclusion: both Calvinists and Arminians can be properly called evangelical since both are part of the same family. John Calvin's reformation in Geneva was quite strictly Calvinist, of course, and his successors were even more strict than he. Those exiles from Britain who had gone to take refuge in Geneva and came back in great numbers to their homeland made Britain a largely Calvinistic country at first. They were in deep protest against the sort of non-Calvinist tendencies that they found within the Anglican church, particularly during the time of James I in the early part of the seventeenth century. They especially despised Archbishop Laud with his Arminian leanings. Yet, if one looks at English history, one finds that there were always those preachers and scholars within it who sought to affirm the idea of divine election. There were others, however, who sought with equal vigor to find more of a place for human freedom. Both contributed in an important sense to the synergistic process by which both divine sovereignty and human responsibility could continue to be affirmed.

In the course of English history, at least during the first 150 years after Calvin, one sees a constant swinging back and forth between a Calvinist and non-Calvinist theology. The Calvinist group in England greatly increased during the 1620s, chiefly in response to Arminian theology and Anglican worldliness. The Calvinistic revolution, called Puritanism, sent large numbers of fervent Christians to America, bearing a kind of Calvinist antipathy to the whole idea of free will and human effort.

I had always thought that the Christian religion was primarily a matter of God's goodness and grace right from the start. While in college, however, I began to discover that other people did not quite see it that way—especially since I also affirmed a belief in the doctrine of sanctification. You see, I was convinced that a person by faith could actually become holy. This, I soon learned, was considered a ridiculous idea by many of my colleagues in college. One of the first good friends I made at the University of Virginia was a staunch Calvinist. The first night of our fledgling friendship, he began his efforts to convert me to his position. I said to my friend, "Let's not argue about religion. I have been so lonely and I am rejoicing so much in just having your friendship, must we argue all the time?" Well, I am glad to report that we did become strong friends. Some twenty years later I went to hear him preach. Following the service, as we talked together, he told me how he had come to a new appreciation for the diversity within the movement which he and I share. We affirmed together how Calvinists and Wesleyans alike are genuinely part of the family.

I have been lecturing recently in colleges of the Church of Christ and the Disciples of Christ, those followers of Alexander Campbell, the Scottish Presbyterian preacher who was active in West Virginia and southwestern Pennsylvania during the early part of the nineteenth century. He founded a community known simply as the Disciples of Christ because he so opposed the divisive nature of denominational Christianity. Of course, the outcome of his effort to try to persuade all Christians to join one community was that he created three new groups: the Disciples of Christ, the Christian Church, and the Church of Christ. These are wonderful Christians—and also part of the evangelical fold. They form an immense community of perhaps five million members in the United States. According to George Gallup, they also profess to being born-again Christians. Yet, most historians continue to overlook the Disciples of Christ when they come to a study of American evangelicalism, despite the fact that their churches dot the landscape of America from Pittsburgh to Abeline.

Given my ardent interest in including these and other little-known groups in the ranks of evangelicalism, you have probably long since begun to wonder how I might go about defining the movement. To those for whom this is true, let me respond that I am using the term to denote those historic American religious communities that are united by a commitment to biblical authority, a belief in the necessity of conversion or new birth, and an emphasis upon worldwide evangelization. Although such a definition has its limitations, to be sure, I am content that it reflects the core teachings of a remarkable movement that unites Arminians and Quakers, Free-will and hard-shelled Baptists, Southern Presbyterians, evangelical Episcopalians, and many others.

Developing Respect for One Another

If this is true, what then is the greatest need among evangelical Christians today? In my estimation, it is the development of respect for one another within the family. The critical and divisive spirit that seems to characterize religious life in America at the end of the twentieth century is destructive to our movement and continues to do great harm. I worried for many years that I might be left out of the club because I possessed simultaneously both too narrow a perspective and too broad a vision. The middle way, as many of you will be all too painfully aware, is often difficult. When I was younger, I often wished I had been born a Presbyterian. Then, I thought, I might have become a banker or a dentist. I could have worn a suit and a tie. My father would not have had to send us out to take care of the cows, I imagined. How wrong in spirit I was to think this way. And how damaging such caricatures can become. To concentrate upon belligerence toward family members, rather than to take up the joyous task of telling people of the love of God in Christ by which they can be saved, seems to me to be both wrongheaded and dangerous.

After all, we are—every one of us—utterly dependent upon God to give us the capacity to hear his truth, to believe and understand his truth, and to respond to his truth with all our hearts so that by faith in the Lord Jesus Christ we can be saved. Grace comes before everything else. And we should pause every day of our lives to thank God for the grace of Christ that reaches us, convicts us of our sins, enables us to truly repent, and frees us from our sins. Some of you, of course, will make adjustments in the way in which such wonderful truths are best articulated; yet, none of us must ever forget the absolute primacy of the grace and goodness of God in our salvation. America is made up of people of many different backgrounds and an array of different inherited theological perspectives. Yet, the truth that unites us is that Jesus Christ died for his fallen creation, that God's love in Jesus Christ can save those who truly repent, and that his Holy Spirit has been given us to lead us in the path toward holiness of heart and life.

In one of his more famous theological addresses, *Addressed to Men of Reason and Religion,* Wesley spoke of the witness of the Spirit. This, for him, was the conscious knowledge of God's forgiving grace in our lives and the power of that same grace through the Holy Spirit to lead us to walk with him and in him until, through the means of grace, we could be led into an experience of inward purity of heart—what Wesley called heart holiness. Although he continued to receive a great deal of criticism

for doing so, Wesley insisted on the centrality and suffi-
ciency of grace. We owe everything to grace, not only for
the instigation of our salvation, but also for the perpetua-
tion of our relationship to God. Wesley used to warn his
preachers who sometimes thought the Lord's Prayer was
not a proper prayer because it had in it "forgive us our
trespasses" and we do not trespass anymore, by telling
them that their "unwitting sins," "sins of omission," and
"sins of ignorance" were so many that they must live day
by day in dependence upon his grace to cover those unwitting and unknown sins.

And so my plea to all of us is that the evangelical community might learn, as John emphasized in the New Tes-
tament, to seek peace with all and to pursue that holiness
of thought and life without which no one can see the Lord.
As the apostle Paul phrased it so many years ago, may
"grace and peace be unto you from God our Father and
the Lord Jesus Christ." How does this happen? What is it
that makes God's grace come to us so that we can repent
of our sins and believe and be led in righteousness and holiness all the rest of our days? It comes, of course, through
the power of the Holy Spirit—the one who lives through
us the life of our Lord Jesus Christ.

When this begins to happen, I am convinced, Christians
become less interested in playing games, less inclined to
cut people out of the kingdom. We become far more interested in including people if we can—be they red or yellow,
black or white, as we used to sing in Sunday school—since
all of God's children are wonderfully precious in his sight.
So when we speak of the task of renewing the evangelical
vision in our time, we must first attend to the crucial task
of breaking down the walls that divide us. We must learn
to follow Jesus' words in John 17: "My prayer is not for
them alone. I pray also for those who will believe in me
through their message, that all of them may be one, Fa-

ther, just as you are in me and I am in you. May they also be in us so that the world may believe that you have sent me. I have given them the glory that you gave me, that they may be one as we are one: I in them and you in me. May they be brought to complete unity to let the world know that you sent me and I have loved them even as you have loved me." This is a lofty standard, of course, and one that often appears overwhelmingly difficult if not impossible. Yet, in God's strength "all things are possible"— and I for one am willing to say, "I do not fully understand why so many others either refuse to agree with my positions or fail to use my language in describing God's glorious truth—but for those who love the Lord Jesus Christ and who seek to live in obedience to God's wonderful Word, I am ready, as John Wesley did so many years ago, to extend a hand of welcome." This, my good friends, is our continuing task and joyous obligation.

Suggestions for Further Reading

Bloesch, Donald. *The Future of Evangelical Christianity: A Call for Unity amid Diversity* (Garden City, N.Y.: Doubleday, 1983).

Bloesch, a Congregationalist who teaches in a Presbyterian seminary, argues that evangelicals should join together to tackle common tasks and not let minor doctrinal differences get in the way of Christian cooperation.

Dayton, Donald W. *Discovering an Evangelical Heritage* (New York: Harper and Row, 1976); "Yet Another Layer of the Onion: Or Opening the Ecumenical Door to Let the Riffraff In." *Ecumenical Review* 40 (January 1988): 87–110.

In *Discovering an Evangelical Heritage*, Dayton suggests that evangelical leaders such as Jonathan Blanchard, Charles Finney, Theodore Weld, and Catherine Booth were at the heart of reform movements such as abolition-ism, feminism, and social welfare. Dayton has long con-tended that the historiography of evangelicals is domi-nated by Reformed and Presbyterian traditions at the expense of those with a Wesleyan, holiness, or Pentecostal perspective. In "Yet Another Layer of the Onion," he asks what it would mean for an ecumenical audience if the bal-ance were redressed.

Hamm, Thomas D. *The Transformation of American Quakerism: Orthodox Friends, 1800–1907* (Bloomington: Indiana Univer-sity Press, 1988).

Filling a gap in the history of American evangelicalism, Hamm chronicles the loss of most of the marks of Quaker distinctiveness through "a combination of internal ten-sions, socioeconomic change, and the influence of non-Quaker religious thought."

Hatch, Nathan O., Mark A. Noll, and John D. Woodbridge, eds. *The Gospel in America: Themes in the Story of America's Evan-gelicals* (Grand Rapids: Zondervan, 1979).

The authors explore the background of seven themes that continue to be important for evangelicals today: theology, the Bible, revivalism, the church, separatism, the nation, and American society. For each of them, the book shows how evangelical attitudes and convictions have been re-lated to American experience—sometimes shaping it, other times being shaped by it.

George Marsden. *Reforming Fundamentalism: Fuller Seminary and the New Evangelicalism* (Grand Rapids: Eerdmans, 1987).

Marsden charts the history of Fuller Theological Seminary from its inception in the late 1940s to the late 1980s, set-ting it in the context of the cultural and religious struggles that helped to define it.

Noll, Mark A., and David F. Wells, eds. *Christian Faith and Practice in the Modern World* (Grand Rapids: Eerdmans, 1988).

With contributions from some of the most respected scholars in the evangelical world, this book speaks both to the discipline of theology and to the ongoing dialogue between Christianity and modern thought. The subjects discussed fall under three main headings: the image of God, the self-disclosure of God, and creation and its restoration.

Wells, David F., and John D. Woodbridge, eds. *The Evangelicals: What They Believe, Who They Are, Where They Are Changing* (Nashville: Abingdon, 1975).

The major themes of who evangelicals are, what they believe, and how they are changing are broken down into subtopics such as the theological boundaries; historical origins; philosophical, scientific, and political thought patterns; and the social-action history of evangelicals.

Index